elizabeth young:
the mind's mess

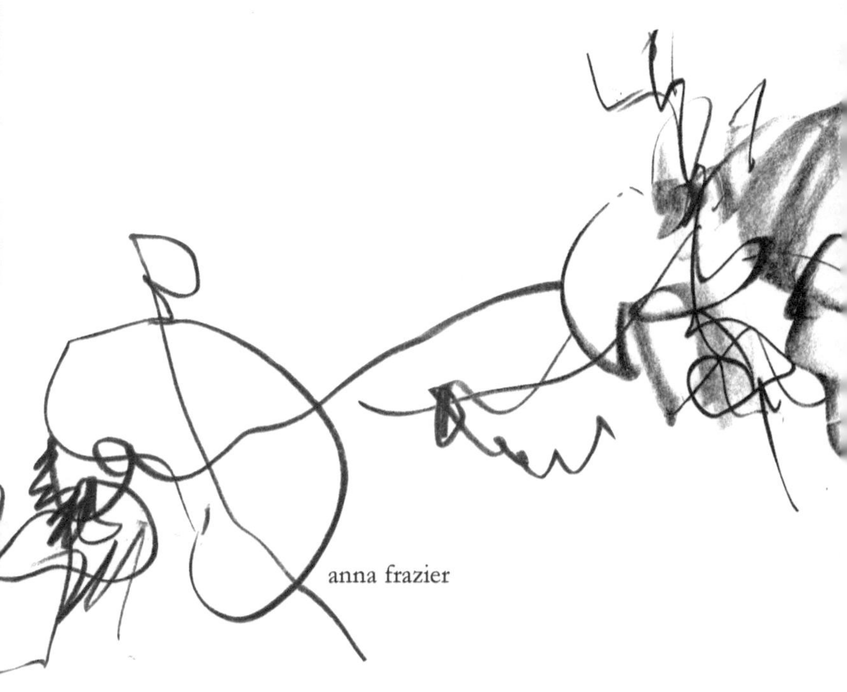

introduction

welcome to the space i created for myself. this book is everything that was true to me at one point in the past. this book is my journey through endless sadness and how poetry is my only way to process tragedy and loss.

this book is not about hope or how to find yourself; it is simply the only explanation i could force out of myself in response to great misfortune.

i wrote this for me, but i also wrote this for the people that wish every book didn't have a happy ending, that just want someone to acknowledge how much they got cheated and how much the world sucks sometimes. this book creates a space that is lacking in our world for people to know that all feelings are valid, to feel them instead of fixing them, and to find understanding through another's most hopeless moments.

if i know anything, it is that trauma scatters a person. life is flung in every direction, becoming complicated with emotions larger than any storm cloud. life gets so filled to the brim with an unfortunate mixture of obligation and desire that every aspect of the mind feels an unsortable jumble. the poems herein are a place to put everything back together — an organization of the mind's mess.

collections:

view other collections at
annafrazierpoetry.com.

connect:

let's talk

visit annafrazierpoetry.com
to subscribe to email updates
on her new collections, view
featured poems, and learn
more about the author.

dedication:

my other halves

let's get a piece
of cake and talk
this over.

note:

the order of things

these books are meant to be read
in order as well as from left
to right. welcome to a new space.

preface:

a popular question

elizabeth young —
who is she?
she is
my inside voice:
the woman who writes.
she is a mixture of
all my secrets
and everything i
wish i could tell you.
she is my truest form,
my purest self,
and
the only person
in this world
that i trust.
she is
my past,
my future,
and the beginning of me
knowing myself...
i finally decided
to let her out.

table of contents

intro:
poems
about
trauma

whatever haunts you

you don't get over it
you don't get past it
time just passes
you get distracted
that's all.

the hole

there is a hole for every trauma,
and after we somewhat recover,
we stay far from that hole
to avoid what may come up out of it.
it is still in our souls,
but we walk around it,
throwing reverence for that darkness
in the general direction
of its residence
without stepping into the hell
that closely awaits us,
should we ever give it more
than an ounce of thought.

the soul's tension

anyone who knows trauma
knows that this hole is
catastrophic and disastrous,
that if we ever dared step,
we might never resurrect.
we who know trauma
build pathways around,
crafting new trails
that somewhat surround
the greatest of pains,
which seek to resound,
but we tell them "No,"
and look at the ground,
remembering fractions
of pains that drown
us up to our ears;
fuck those who say
we have nothing to fear.

stepping in

i have entered this hole —
sometimes i fall in.
it's not ever my choice;
common words push me in.
i see two paths:
there's one without people,
in which no one can last,
and one with many people,
of which not one will last.
this is the first and kindest hole;
it leads to other, less-kind holes.
the holes further down the path,
i have found, don't give two roads,
but one, in which i drown
further and further
under the world's hatred.
trauma loves me, i tell you,
and nothing can change it.

the one i fell in today

i drive past you
two times a week.
i see the dark tan of
your freckled face.
sometimes,
if you are close enough,
i see them — poison-green eyes.
but if you are too far for that,
i only see your golden hair.
i don't want to remember
the way your lips were always chapped
or the smushed-oval shape of your fingers,
but their existence is branded onto my brain
from all the heat and pressure forced on me
against the department store, dressing-room door.

hole 2

there is just darkness,
no light in this hole.
there is shame and regret and grief
in this hole.
this is just one hole
out of many holes in my soul.
this hole is called Rape;
i will never be whole.

something about me

i seem to attract trauma
and toxins.
the people with problems —
they seek me;
they want in.
they know i will fix them
by taking them on,
by swallowing their problems
and making them mine.
they know i will love them
minus the limits.
they know, at every cost,
i will find them their fixings.

the result

a person grows weary
from having less soul;
souls don't grow back
or get bigger
or full.
many holes make one crawl
into them faster —
then one doesn't move
for fear of disaster.

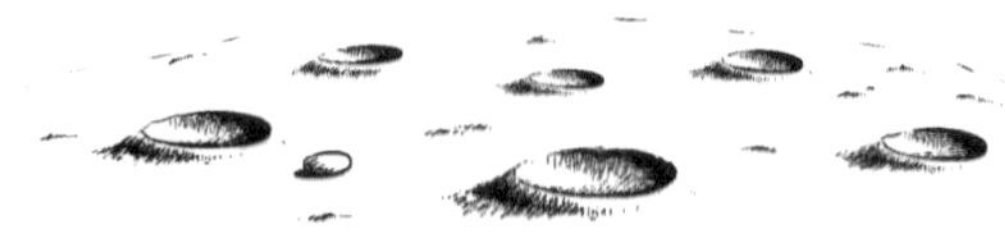

disillusion, resolution

trauma,
pain,
cancer,
loss —
all of you write your words on my life,
but i will erase them with my own hands.
even so, a faint mark will be left.
then i wonder:
has my whole life
been a symptom
of trauma
or medication —
who am i,
and
how do i find myself?
i must learn to be my own friend,
to be at peace with my own company.

aftermath of trauma

i think,
in the aftermath of trauma,
people latch onto anything
that gives them life,
even if it's for the wrong reasons,
even if they know it's not meant to be,
even if it's dangerous.

"you've developed unhealthy habits,"
others shout.
"i'm just trying to survive,"
i scream
from the jail cell
of my dying soul.

abduction

even today i had happiness
like a bird in my hand
but i could barely see
the iridescent glow on its wings
or hear its heavenly song
because trauma was so
   violently
      present
instead of me;

another gorgeous moment
taken.

yoga

the stretch
unlocked the many cases
i thought i'd secured;
it found the varied traumas
i thought i'd stuffed tightly
into their places.
in my back
it found the rape,
and in my chest it found her death;
my shoulders held the lack of my father,
but my knees carried the pain of heartbreak.

stained, tattered, living room chair

why is it so comfortable
to sink into the
panic
and
damage?

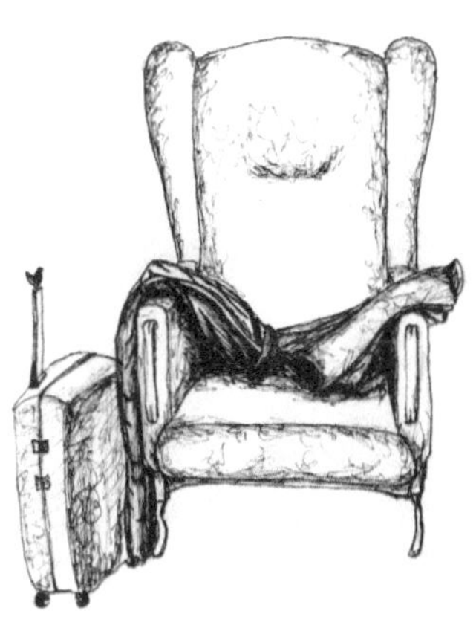

heart of many colors

which is preferable:
a cloudy sky or clear?
a blanket of blue
or dollops of puffy white,
unpredictably exasperated?
some of the greatest masterpieces
of our time
are quite a mess themselves.
so, why is my internal chaos
any less desirable
than her blanket of blue?

losing
aunt:

missing
her

i grieve still

she was a starving figure, a shell.
when i held her, she was gone.
when i felt her hand, it was not there.
it was her body i touched,
but she was absent,
because cancer simplified her brain.
she used to call me Pumpkin and
laugh in that special way.
i don't remember that sound anymore,
but i remember holding her body
and how it got smaller every time.

unfortunately

this poem has been removed
due to the requests
of the writer's family.

in place, please accept a summary:
this poem described the effect that
cancer has on the physical body
and the way nothing can prepare
a person to view a loved one
in an extreme condition.

a remnant of the poem:

she was no longer a woman
that shared my blood and memories.
now, she was just a woman.

what i didn't know well

a mother
of overflowing love,
the life of the party,
a library-going,
picnic-having,
bright woman —
sharp
but so funny.

last words

i love you, sweetheart
i love you too.

interruption

no one here was there
no one knows what i saw
my inside collapses
i feel no happiness
her memory shouts quietly
in my direction

i screw up my good days
with bad memories
bad memories are a familiar place
being sad is my safe place
i go back to that place
to find myself
because that's where i lost myself
that's where we all lost
ourselves
and left our souls and her
bones

i remember hearing her
lungs
fill
with liquid

hearing her
struggle
to
live
and she all at once —

unfortunately

this poem
has been removed
due to the requests
of the writer's family.

in place, please accept
a summary:
this poem described
the effect that
watching someone
die had on the writer
and how beautiful
it was for only one
minute before the pain
of the loss was felt.
the poem also described
the way that cancer
changed the woman's
physical body but
never her happiness,
demonstrating
the woman's
strength.

a remnant of the poem:

death ripped me apart.
death ruined me.
death poisoned me.
death took my happiness.
[...]
but cancer never took
her happiness.

the morning after

it is june twenty-seventh;
it is dawn.
my feet are anvils;
you are gone.

seven years i stood near
the side of your bed
where i could hear
every breath,
every cough,
and then your death.

moving's unnecessary;
my journey has ended;
my purpose at all
is now expended.

i miss you

grief is the sun:
it never stops rising.

happy birthday

at this rare moment,
when wildflowers bloom
and summer storms fly in,
when i am troubled
but calmer than the ocean,
when i am curious
but feel no obligation
to create a problem
or fix one,
how my thoughts are contented
upon such an unprophesied accident:
it is the twenty-ninth of april.

the
darkness
that
awaited

new reality

night after night
sobs, wails, tears
they were endless

my middle is broken

i can hear myself
struggling to breathe.
i can feel the pain
in every part of my body.
dragging my feet along,
it hurts so much just
to take one step.
to sit for long hurts too.
i can't bike today;
my middle is broken.
i can't breathe deeply,
but i need to stay alive.
i want to cry,
but my middle is broken,
and that might make it
hurt worse.

a canyon

this tile floor is cold
and familiar,
and i am lost —
not with alcohol
or medications,
just the incredible
and terrible power
of human sadness.

anna frazier

i'm sorry for the look
i have on my face

trauma and tragedy,
even the opposite —
these are big things.
big things change
deeper layers of a person's soul
than ones that emotion
can affect or reflect.
big things change
a person's default —
the look on their face.
i am not angry;
nothing is wrong;
i do not feel unwell —
this is just my face.

too dark

it's hard to smile
most of the time
i smile for you
because i don't want to be
too dark

anna frazier

raven

tie your lips
tie them shut
let a rose grow
but never cut
your ribboned lips
don't speak
your eyes look
but can't see
lungs burn
a twisted song
the moon shines
the night is long
blue dark
on a dark rose
a blue song
no one knows
raven knows it
oh so well
he sings this tune
in silent swell
swell is silence
to those who listen

blackest rose
turn an ear
to prudent prose
careful, dear stem
lest you snap
only a moment
and you're trapped
the careful raven
watches you
forget not
that night watches too
careful, rose
of your burnt tips
that you don't end
blackened and in rips
the ribbon's ease
is a ribbon's ties
the ribbon loves
to paralyze lips tied
with twinkle-less woes
cry for star shine
raven goes

darkness hides people

light does not exist,
only darkness.
motivation died;
it lays cold
on the floor of my soul.
i don't care to bury it —
its absence entirely would kill me.
even the roses are dark today.
the sun has set inside and out,
but my soul does not sleep.
help!
i sink into the blackest of wells;
this well convinces me
that i want to dive deeper.
i'm not empty yet,
just full of darkness.
but, the love of darkness
is terrifying and satisfying.
it weighs me down;
it convinces me that
darkness is the safest,
even safer than the light
of the sun or an evening lamp.
hiding, endless hiding.

what depression does

ocean around me
ocean within
ocean is velvet
on top of my skin
chained to the depths
light is miles upward
oxygen
a distant memory.

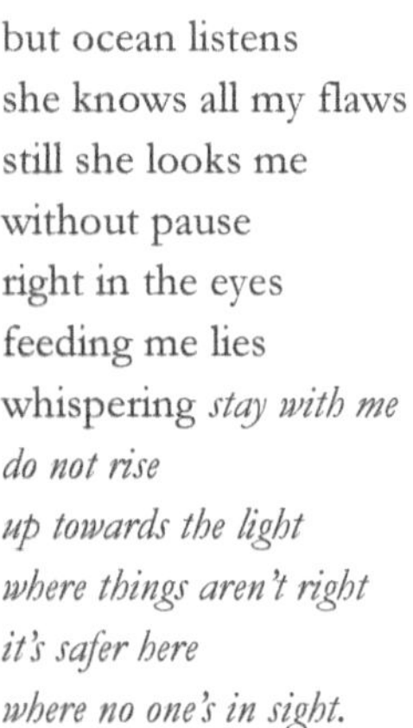

but ocean listens
she knows all my flaws
still she looks me
without pause
right in the eyes
feeding me lies
whispering *stay with me*
do not rise
up towards the light
where things aren't right
it's safer here
where no one's in sight.

an enveloping body
a calming embrace
enticing me
into her space
she is Fear turned to Apathy
i don't want to escape.

ocean — my constant
companion.

stagnant pond

i
am a stagnant pond.
refuse on the bank
makes me unappealing.
the smell of waste
is a fog over my head;
the clouds cannot even
see me.
everyday i bubble up
through the fog
just to catch a few drops
of contaminated oxygen.
seasons roll on;
i am unchanged.

dry me up,
take what you can
for your own use.
it is better that my reeds
be used to make fine music
than to cloud any view
of heaven;
for, life is to be enjoyed,
not simply tolerated.

tired of living

everything that i do
has no return
and i am
being perpetually emptied
but never filled again
tell me how
i am supposed to keep
on living for everyone
else then
you only live once
so i'll die for myself
not them.

exhausted routine

i'm tired of laughing
just to get through another day
knowing tomorrow will hold today's troubles
the same way today held yesterday's.

acceptance

the worst part about
wanting to kill yourself
is knowing that if you did
you'd be letting everyone else down
except yourself.

paralyzed maybe

could move
maybe
if i tried
but nothing in me
wants to try
at all.
top face of
the bed sheet
is safer than
anything outside
these four walls.

try to understand me

nauseation: a condition
not remedied by medication,
not fixable by recreation,
or treated by capacitation.
this fever feels like suffocation —
can i reach abbreviation?
i come to the realization
there is no amelioration
except for the annihilation
of my throat — regurgitation!

stop.

find in your imagination
a similar situation:
anxiety is nauseation
of the soul — disintegration,
everyday anticipation
of my heart's asphyxiation
not remedied by medication,
or fixable by recreation,
not treated by capacitation.
i can't reach abbreviation;
there is no amelioration
except for the annihilation
of myself — assassination!

raspberry jam

anxiety is a swamp monster
that creeps up on you
and drapes over your skin
like a pouring of raspberry jam
cloaking you in a sticky goo
suffocating you until
tears break through

stop and go

the only way out is through
that's what they say
but i am shaking
and gasping
between each breath
the closet floor is too cold
for my weak body
but i don't have the energy
to make myself any warmer or
to cry through the trauma more
so i'll freeze
and silence will shroud
my fetal form
but the tears will always
keep moving.

blindness

with blood on my cracked lips,
i blink just to see the shifting path.
my future is as certain as a spider's web,
my days slower than a weed grows.
nothing seems to hold my attention,
and, like a locust before molting,
my anxiety turns within me —
it agitates my stomach lining
and burns holes in my head.

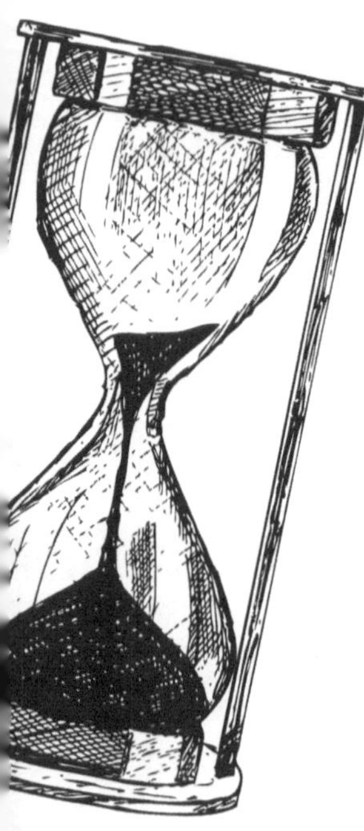

endless thursdays

i don't like saturdays.
saturdays are the days
where i am forced to face
every sadness i have put off
in the weekdays.
maybe we could get rid
of saturdays
and just have endless
thursdays instead.

the dream

i don't necessarily
want to be
something great
or a name on
everyone's tongue;
one of my largest aspirations
is to not be so lonely
for even just a day.

a deal with the devil

they always say
to chase your dreams
but never ask
that if it means
a piece of you dies
is it still worth it?

dust to dust

i don't know how to "process"
rape
i don't know how to "deal with"
death
i don't know how to "understand"
my father
i don't know how to "be patient"
with heartbreak

my throat closes up
and i wonder
what's the point of anything
if it all burns in the end?

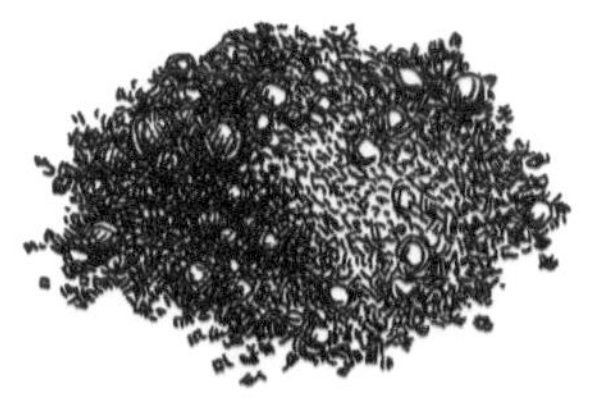

migraine ii

a hundred miles deep,
diamonds form
by a crushing heap
of carbon and ore.
repurposed atoms,
numerous and reborn,
are birthed by time
with endless return.

migraines are like this,
but flashbacks replace
the role of the carbon,
and you are faced
with many memories
that, over time,
if suppressed,
will combine
to form a heavy,
crushing weight
of emotional atoms
there to stay
inside the brain
where they wait
to be mined like diamonds;
but it's too late.

fear of existence

i don't even know
what i'm afraid of anymore.
nothing matters enough
for me to be afraid of it,
but without warning,
everything hurts.
what's the purpose
in putting me together
if i know i'll be
so easily destroyed
again,
again,
again.

well?

when i am not thinking anything

the briars in the patches
are happier than i.
even on my good days,
they attack innocent bystanders.
they prowl in cotton
and desire to prick
the fingers of any
who get caught in the thicket.

what is the point
of everything

you are my point
at the end of everything
if the only reason
i am here
is to make sure you
are okay
then i will live
for that.

losing
dad:

the dad
i knew

fond memory

in my mind, i see that picture of us —
that picture with my fluffy jacket,
the fish in my hand,
the first fish i ever caught.
you, a mustache, are my best friend,
and i am Joy in your arms,
a pink snowman.

i am four

you let me
eat ice cream for breakfast,
cut my own hair,
and buy a real easter bunny;
said you'd find a small horse
to celebrate my birthday.
you are simple to me:
endlessly genius,
happy for miles,
and more carefree than
the wind itself.
oh, how life wears on a person.

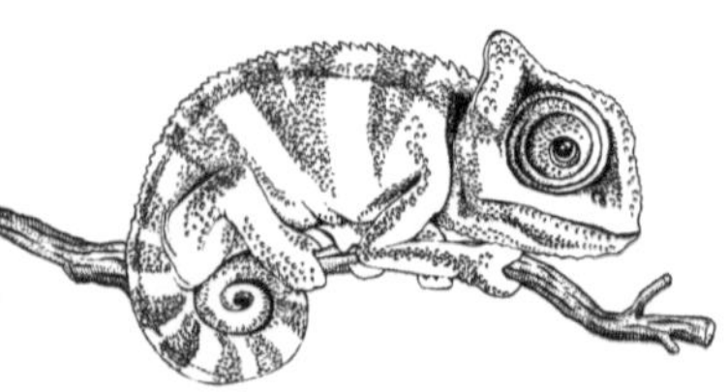

unstable

before seventeen,
i couldn't imagine
a different way with you
except to be
your closest companion.
but
how suddenly it all changed.
how suddenly you were quieted —
how suddenly did we no longer
discuss the reason stars float in darkness
or the way that rainbows can't be touched.
how suddenly i began to ask myself
everyday:
will today be like yesterday,
or will today be the day
that you change
again?

you are just like me

before,
we often talked of how
misunderstood we felt
in this world,
how loud noises
and lots of people
make us uncomfortable.
and then
each night,
i see you disappear
to sort through
your pain
where no one will see you.
i realize,
for the second time,
that you are just like me.

the dad
trauma knew

and it haunts me: a series

I
i am seventeen.
we are all quiet,
and everything is melting,
but i am still yours.
suddenly,
you lose it —

you're right, dad.
i didn't see your mother
leave this world.
no, i will never understand
what it is to not have a mother.

but here, in this moment,
i do not have a father.

II
there are four.
then blinding anger
and white faces.
dad leaves,
and there are three.
door slams;
two saw everything.
where is dad going?
waiting, endless waiting.

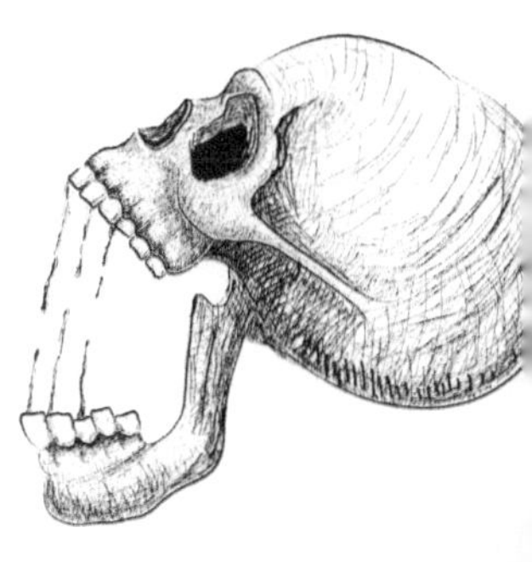

III
this is shocking —
this is uncomfortable —
am i still yours?
in all of ten minutes,
at the intersection of my maturity
and your PTSD,
i became to you a dart board
instead of a person.
it's been three years since that;
i liked it better before.

a mess

after you spill
your trauma all over me,
do i wash me first
or you?

will it ever be like it used to?

you say it's a pleasure to watch your children
grow into this or that,
to change their bad habits into good ones,
to stretch themselves,
etc.
yet, your sickness has overtaken you.
so,
step no closer to me,
and let your pleasure be that you watch me grow
from over there.

ice water

i will drink this water
until i drown
if it means
i don't have to speak more words
to you.
i will drink this water;
it will fill my lungs.
the cold river will freeze me
from the inside out.
but still,
that is a better feeling
than the one i get
from forcing any conversation.

half a glass

half a glass
i have drunk
so far,
an anomaly
for any evening of mine,
but to fill my mouth
with cold, flavorless liquid
is preferred
to filling it
with flavorless words.

under my breath

i'm allowed to be unpleasant
without attaching my mood
to a mental health problem.

"where are you?"

you ask me.
i slip from here
into a world
of yesterday's nightmares —
i think of all the times
your anger has scarred me.
so gentle a person you are,
but every so often,
your power hurts.
you examine me as i consider what to say
and how to tell you in the nicest way
i don't like you anymore.

how do i sit

how do i sit
cordially in a room
with two people
who were so deeply
involved in my
greatest destruction?

protecting myself

what is it in me
that won't forgive you,
that won't let you shine
like the brilliant light that you are?
you try so hard to repair
what's broken,
but i've decided
somewhere,
in the tens of times
that i myself have tried
to repair what is broken,
that i do not have it in me
to restore after the storm,
so i keep my distance.
am i protecting myself
or just hurting us more?

you finally spoke

"You and I
used to sit,
to walk
for hours,
to talk about
all of life.
We were as close
as two people could be.
This chasm between us
is no indication
of overturned hearts
or love lost.
You love me endlessly.
I love you endlessly.

We are okay.

One day, we will
gaze at the stars
again;
one day we will
solve world peace."

losing
him, him, and
him:

many men

roses

i put roses on my cheeks for you,
but you still chose her.
i pulled the petals of daisies for you,
but you still chose her.
i lit the blood of sapphires for you,
but you still chose her.
i had something i wrote for you,
but you still chose her.

long distance

i am there.
you and i are a new puzzle.
all our edges meet:
our sentences, our eyes,
our fingers, our minds.
everything snaps,
not in one way or two;
we are one thousand
tiny pieces —
a magnificent hue.

and then i return
to begin my work
in another life,
another world.
pieces are lost
along my travel.
puzzle edges
turn so jagged.
they don't fit together
the way they had when
from two feet away,
i touched your mind's skin.

here i am,
far from home,
falling for someone
i barely know.
where did all
our pieces go?

i wonder too

don't say something you can't take back.
i think i'm falling for you too,
but sometimes i don't know.

anna frazier

is falling a choice?

there's a point
at which you feel yourself
falling in the silence
of the cold night
with drips
of country music, and
you have to ask yourself
if it's worth it to fall.
do you let yourself
drown in the atmosphere,
or do you scoot yourself
to the left a little
away from his body
away from that warmth
just to prove to yourself
that falling
is a choice?

why can't we be honest

things were casual
until they weren't.
now i can't call
just to laugh.
now i have to
have a reason,
maybe wait
one whole season,
to hear your voice
in hopes of
looking "independent."

fever

falling for you
feels just like a fever
i am hot
and uncomfortable
and out of control

secrets worse than a knife

all that i want in the whole world
is for you to hold me
and tell me how safe i am in your arms.
the worst part is not the knife
of the unknown, the possiblity of
the unsafety, but how many
of these thoughts i must hide from you.

pinot noir

swimming in the vast oceans
of blood and lust
to have you
is a must
wine can make you
fall in love
i swear

correction

i l o v e y o u
no i don't

anna frazier

the *overthinker*

it was not instinctive,
the way i fell for you.
it was not like
an intake of breath.
it was logical, calculated,
and it took everything i had
to stop it from happening.
but my methods failed,
for, the parts of me
that want to reach far forward
are thwarted (almost)
by the parts that want to reach
far, far, far back.

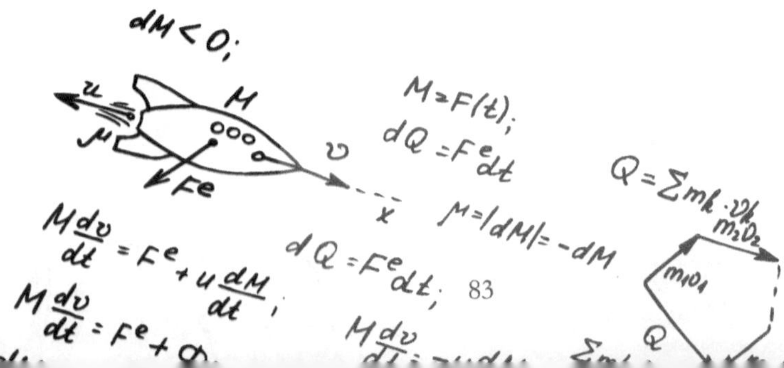

83

abuse

brown eyes, green eyes.
what color are they?
i see you in my dreams,
but eyes open,
i see tears and screams.
in just three days,
you make your mark.
there and gone,
you fly fast — a lark.
you are good to me,
my dreams are saying.
i am there with you each night,
feeling you beneath dim lights.
you are sweet; that smoke you made
was not the reason i obeyed.
you tower high over my nineteen.
at twenty-four, you make me seem
unreasonable, silly, just a pretty face.
ignoring me, you seem sincere,
"just focused, dear." you call me
things, but i stay near.
hands over mouth,
i cannot laugh.
your commands over me —
why these schemes
did you craft? i finally decide
i am a waste of your time
because you tell me so.
with that cigarette, you tell me to go
away from you, forever, go
away and never come back, so
i leave you on the sidewalk there,
and in the night i sit where
we used to say, "com'é stai"

and sweet, little words that
all were lies.
a halo around you,
i saw a glow
covering up
what you did not show.
all the dirty ways you used me,
somewhere inside,
i knew you abused me,
but outside my heart,
they were too hard to find:
the truths that could have saved me
from being confined
by dark, dark memories.

one good day

the wind was blowing
a summer night
both of us lay staring into the other's eyes
the stars gazed at us for once
he said "what's on your mind"
i couldn't tell him
so i paused forever
"i'm falling for you"
i said and he said
"can't you see i'm falling for you too?"

falling in love with you instead of myself

i'm honestly so petrified to lose you
that i can't even breathe
do you know how confusing it is
to act like i don't care
when you're everything
i've ever wanted

doubts

can i talk for a minute
about how much i want
everything that you are
and at the same time how
when i finally get you
i seem to self sabotage

what if i just want
someone
instead of you

universal

i think we're all lonely
i think we all just want
someone to
talk to
trust
be ourselves
with.

an unhealthy habit

i want to give
all my damaged pieces to
someone,
someone
that will keep them all together,
one person that will
stay
instead of going
because people are constantly
going;
no one
ever

stops

to be there
for somebody
except themselves,

and sometimes,
they can't even do that.

damage

half of me says,
please, no,
and
this will hurt,
but the other half
says,
let's try again,
and
maybe he's changed,
and
he's not as bad as
your last boyfriend,
a rapist.
that's what rape will do
to your standards —
it will make anything
that is not rape
seem okay
because at least
it's not
   that
    bad.

scared to love

coffee was warm &
puppies were furry;
it wasn't the rain
that made my hearing blurry.
trauma was silently
screaming in my ear,
so intensely
that i could barely hear
the words you were saying or
the music that was playing.
all i could think of
was my heart weighing
the impossible cost
of a friendship with you.
it could be everything,
or even worse,
nothing at all,
and then i would fall
for the thousandth time
down into that hole.
what does true love mean
at all?

everything's upside down

i thought i loved you
i think i still do
or at least i remember
what that made me happy about you

i think i'm sad
that i talked to you today
that you found a way into my life
despite efforts to keep you away

you were persistent against my resistance
now i must be permanent
on keeping you out
but
it's not that far
from the mountain
to the valley.

burn the ships

there comes a point
where we decide
whether we're moving
forward or backward,
whether we're going to
burn the ships
or board them,
but can we do both
at the same time?

history repeats itself

you speaking to me
reminds me of everything.
my soul turns the other way;
my heart pleads, *please, don't stay.*
my stomach growls in aching pain.
everything in me says you're the same,
but love is strong —
it holds me down,
it sticks and glues
my feet to the ground,
trapping my soul, my heart,
and that sound
coming from my stomach
all to the round
surface of you:
old, but still new.

a secret

i don't like
cold hands or cold feet,
at least when they're mine.
but i like yours.

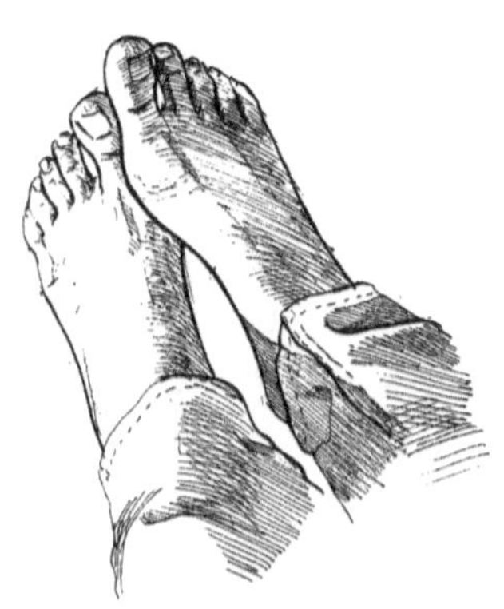

a game

let's pretend,
i say to myself,
let's pretend
the past is erased,
words that preface
an unwise decision
and inevitable pain.

let's pretend you are
giving instead of taking,
winning instead of losing,
loving instead of lusting,
shining instead of burning,
healing instead of hurting.

i wasn't ready

i was small but stable,
at least as stable as a daisy.

but, if a breeze is strong enough,
even if the daisy is rooted deeply
in the dirt, the daisy wilts —
it even flies from its roots into the sky
with all the other damage
in this world.

i sigh, *don't play with my feelings.*

to you

please forget i exist
please forget i am here
don't remember me
don't fill up whatever space in your head
with me
don't invite me to your house
and please
don't call me
you don't remember me when i'm gone
so please forget me when i'm here

forest fire

"should we run
to the mountains?"
i ask, and you say,
"we can't see them.
we'll stay here, okay?"

"let's run from this fire,"
i tell you, "don't play."

you shout, "who cares,
sweetheart, which way.
through the flames,
through the trees,
through the ashes,
brush, and leaves.
maybe the mountains,
maybe not. don't touch
the fire — it's real hot."

and i say to you,
"we're turning blue.
this smoke has choked

us all the way through.
please, to the mountains,
can we run?"

you say, "shh — don't
think too much."

i stomp out
your cigarette
and flee toward
the snow-fire mountains.
your nonchalance
floats through
embered air, and
cracks of tree snaps
make love with
the click of your lighter
flowing again.

i run, and a bit of fire
kisses my hair.

fire has two sides

but
there is a little piece of my heart
that will love him for a very long time —
not forever, but
just for a long time,
because he was the light
at the end of a very dark tunnel.
i found out after some time
that the light i was seeing when i looked at him
was the warm and inviting light
of a crackling fire.
coming closer,
i realized that fire
burns, destroys, and eliminates,
that instead of sunshine at the end of the tunnel,
i walked into a forest fire.

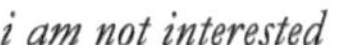

i am not interested

i am not interested
in talking or catching up.
tell me how much i mean to you.
do i mean everything?
because if i am anything less
than everything to you,
then i am not enough.

all is temporary

i'm afraid you'll disappoint me
again,
but then,
humiliation is a temporary feeling.

space

the space between
our shoulders
tells me
everything
to write about you.
hours later,
here i am
on the closet floor
again,
weak at the weight
of feeling too much.

your voice

my heart races at your voice;
it's like gunshots in my ears —
i hear it and duck
for fear of getting pierced.
i examine my own body,
looking for a bullet.

did you shoot me?

was i wounded?

your voice ii

when i hear your voice,
i think of heartbreak,
mistakes,
and unclean breaks.
when i hear your voice,
i'm filled with war,
hiding, and fear.
you are a coyote;
i am a small hare.
i run as fast as i can,
but you will always catch me.

lions, tigers

i am the lion;
you are the tiger.
we meet, we mate,
laughter ensues,
confusion enters,
stands between us,
an ugly monster.
i know two things:
we are too wild
to exist around each other,
and i can always
tell the future.

what kind of party are you throwing

you throw compliments out
like confetti
and give love away
like a party favor,
but for some reason,
everyone that leaves your party
isn't happy
at all.

you are a rainbow

i thought it was nice at first
that joy came from the corners
of your eyes like stardust,
and the way you shine made me think
nothing could put out that light.
but upon closer inspection,
you are a rainbow:
enticing at first glance,
except there's nothing to hold onto.
you're so busy trying to be every color
that i fall into the puddle
of your falsehood.

before, i had hope

you even fail yourself sometimes.
how did i expect
you not to fail me too?

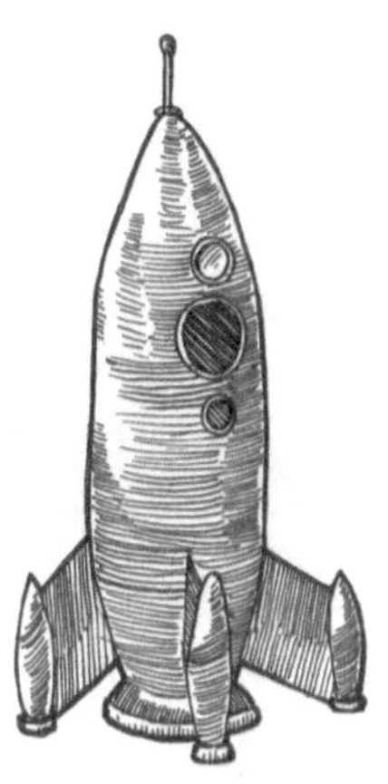

invisible bruises

someone who doesn't constantly lie
while swearing he's telling the truth —
that would be enough.

you are the sun

i look at you
for moments and moments,
my eyes burning more
every second that i spend
on your dangerous face,
and out of all the things
you did to me,
or everything
you never did for me,
the way you never looked
back at me
in all those moments
haunts me the most.

handle with care

the sun rose
and holiday came
took my ten
and sat in silence
dropped a vase
and stepped on thin ice
my bones snapped
when he made a promise
all these fragile things
but i broke instead

horizon

someday,
i'll move away.
you won't see me,
and i won't see you —
what a dream.
i hope
someday
comes quick.

what i've learned

to trust a man
is suicide.
how many times
have i killed myself?

stinger

i have found
that the root of all suffering
is attachment
so ask me again
why i have no interest in love

tired of getting hurt

i think i like it
better over here,
seeing you run
here and there,
watching
a stranger's life.
i don't want to know you;
there's always a knife.

stay where i never knew you.
i'm safer over here.

jaded

i don't want anything
with anyone anymore.
being in love is such a powerless feeling.
today, i have power;
tomorrow, it may pack up and leave.
but right now,
i will soak up the feeling
of not missing anyone
or anything
and just being here with myself.
maybe i'm jaded,
or hardened,
or hopeless,
but at least i have power.

things i tell myself

1. they do exist.
2. focus on yourself.
3. you don't need them.
4. it's almost over.
5. memories
are not an invitation
to be triggered.

evening thoughts

for maybe the second or third time,
i am happy without you.
hot water is an embrace from oneself.
it is a peaceful and comforting feeling,
even hopeful
when i am content without you.
it is a much needed relief
from the incessant and strong feeling
of missing you.

silver on the wind

for a brief moment,
i caught your scent in a draft,
and i breathed in
every last drop of the air
that surrounded me
until it was gone.

what ended us

i love you,
i just don't like you anymore.

fly me to the moon by frank sinatra

i don't even realize
it's playing
until it springs into my ears
(a crow hopping and shrieking)
until i feel it slip down
into my heart
and it hurts from the inside out
(a rat-baby's fingers tremble)

i remember he sang it to me
in the dark
i was crying
again
he sang it to me
imperfectly
he brushed his fingers
through my tangled hair
and held me until i stopped
how many times
did he put me back together
with an old song
when i thought
certainly
he is my future

i get up and leave
i don't want to hear the rest
but it still tumbles in my ear drums
it still pushes out from my heart
(a foal in its mother's stomach
pressing all the edges)

exhausted from feeling so much

it's this great weight
in the pit of my stomach —
sometimes it gets lighter,
sometimes heavier.

your absence is always there,
but you aren't,
and in every way,
i feel that.

a few of my favorite things

in particular order:
wildflowers
a thunderstorm
winter wind
a crackling fire
the way coffee smells
the middle of the ocean
the lack of tension
any unlonely moment
understanding
escape

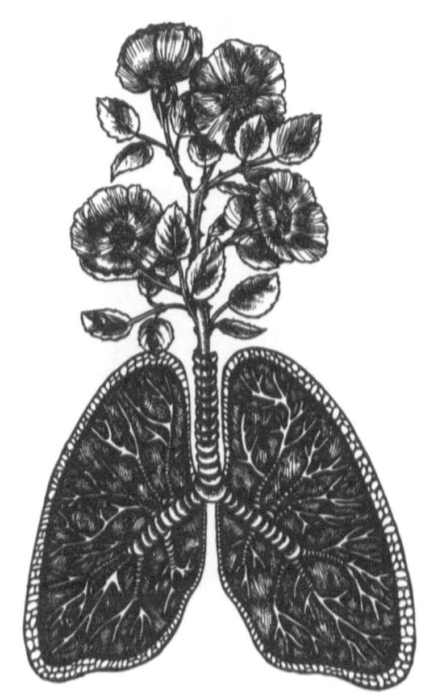

breathe in

feel the air fill you
without ache.
that is the antithesis of pain;
that is what it is
to not miss someone.

while running

nothing can replace the feeling
of not missing someone.
it is a feeling i am feeling
more often everyday,
a feeling that says
i am okay.

the long winter
to my first love

prelude: forgotten after separation

you think everything is okay.
you are busy building fires
and gathering food to sustain yourself
during this long winter.
but what do you think i'm doing
while you're hunting and gathering?

a forest: above and below

the long winter holds you, a forest creature: a great blue heron. you are strong, tall, and beautiful. your wings are broad and round, and your legs trail well beyond your tail plume. with feathers kind to the skin, you're striking to the eyes. you stand motionless on the bank, poised and still. you are a constant in a world of chaos.

the long winter holds me too: a gingerbread fawn with snow-spots. i bring joy to onlookers when they glimpse me in the shadows. i am small and bony, my legs toothpicks against my spine. shaking and restless, i crawl under your wing. it is night.

if i were green, i'd be a dandelion — it has many gifts to give, and others like to take from it. many pick it up from the root and pull away at its seeds just to see the wind blow. they then discard it; it's left for the birds — lifeless but generous always.

if you were green, you'd be moss. moss is trustworthy, soft, and never harmful. it is a comforting kind of green that isn't easy to find — only in the damp forests. moss-clumps in the forest are unobtrusive, not taking from anyone and not forcing their way to the top, like tyrannical ivy vines.

in the valley, you'd be water. you're stable, clear-minded, and life-giving. you're noble, patient, and understanding — water too. if water is left in a glass unattended, it won't grow tired of the air the way that milk does. it will simply be there, still, where it was left. it will not ask why you've been away or where you went, but instead, it will go to all the places in your body that need life, and it will restore you.

in the valley, i would be the runoff from a coffee bean. coffee stirs inside of a person like poison. no one can see the energy that furls in the liquid, that lurches backward and forward, invisibly active. it isn't natural but a product of humanity. it poisons the forest, not nutritious for the vegetation. how ironic that the forest bore this small seed, but it's humanity that made it toxic.

oh, heron, do you remember when you and i were seeds, when we asked the raindrops our questions? we inquired if we'd grow to be tall or short and if we'd be green or some other color. we asked each other what we might do if we ever came at odds. you said we would ask the sun, and i agreed, not thinking we'd ever be at odds. But here today, at odds we are, and it's my turn to ask of you, "what should we do with the odds that have come between you, me, and our childhood selves?"

water belongs in the forest, but i am coffee, a foreigner — i don't belong, not anymore. i used to be pure like water, but humanity's twist has polluted me. i am poison to the place you live. i'm unknown to you after all this time; i'm misunderstood, and i confuse the natural order of things. once i was a part of your forest, a product of my childhood tree, but now that the world has taken and remade me, i am nothing like my first self. do you think i can become a part of your forest again? do you think i can undo the damage that has been done to me by this world, or do you think i am unchangeable?

even so, moss, all i want is to be in the forest alone with you where no one can see us — where i can look at you, where you can see my soul, the one you knew before my lion-petals dried up. i hope you still see that beauty instead of just what's left over. my outside might be less, but my character is maintained; i might look different, but i still feel the same.

forlorn

in the forest, a heron: indigo
and white with a high neck
and observant eyes. he holds
wisdom and stability. he sees
everything. he personifies beauty.
his legs are longer than years,
his beak stronger than
the human spirit.

an oblivious fawn makes her
way through the trees. the heron
sees her shadow reach the edge
of the riverbank. the fawn's wide eyes
admire the heron's colors as they flee
from her in a flash. she watches
his graceful strength fly away,
and her crown falls.

underneath the willow tree,
the fawn leans against her bones
and weeps. i am the fawn, you are
the heron, my bones are poetry.

abandonment

i want to run as fast
as i can into the safety
of a bear's arms.
i say a bear, because
a bear is not safe,
especially a wild bear.
so when you say
you are not sure
if you love me,
i want to run fast
into the arms of a bear,
because even that feels safer
than your uncertainty.

semi-appearance

now i have a question for you:
what would happen if you had
a bear for a pet?

say you had a bear for a pet,
and one day understood
that the bear must be set free
for the health of both you
and the bear.

so you let it go, and one day
find the bear wounded
in the forest.

you ask the bear, "are you okay?"
and the bear shakes her head
no.

then, is it okay to care
for the bear, to take the bear
under your wing if you have
no intention of welcoming
her back into your home?

wolves

quiet — the wolves will hear you. i will tell you in the shelter of this naked canopy as the moon leans on us: you are busy hunting and gathering for what will sustain you in the long winter. i think you know the winter is long, so you hop and fly at any disturbance. what's missing is a fawn's grace, a trait that once accompanied you. the fawn understands she must step slowly and not overthink. if the fawn overthinks, she may linger in open spaces for a moment too long and be spotted by the wolves.

do not let yourself be spotted by the wolves. do not overthink or stay in open spaces for too long. do not even allow your mind to wander to the darkest places of your intelligence, for boredom is the devil's playground, and that is where the wolves lie.

frost

something i drank? was it that cold water from the hole near the stream?

you showed me a hole with a stream running through it for us to drink from, but the water from that river has poisoned us. it's bitter; i'm coughing — the long winter holds up clean water in glaciers, so that i must dig to find anything to drink. you are not the strong one i once thought you to be; for now, your wings touch the forest floor, and feathers from many years are as flakes of snow.

where are you? i call for you, but all i hear is a quiet ambivalence toward your past and future.

my organic frame cannot process this kind of pain. i don't know how to be without you; my life is full, but my heart is empty. there is not even time for us to wander the forest together, but i would find it if i could.

me without you is like an illness, an everlasting disease. it creeps through my veins, ever looking for my heart. like frost, closing the safe passages to my soul, it continues to crawl. i am terrified it will find my heart and freeze that too. i remember when we were young and vowed to always stay together… i am still here, only having left you for a brief moment to see the world outside, but you left
too and never returned.

i stand out by the trees and wait for you,

myself frozen from the inside out. i am unable to move — the ice has reached my inner ring. i am eternally stuck looking for you.

i know this winter will not last forever, but i am not wholly certain it will leave me unaffected — like frostbite, the endings of it damage the nerve endings, resulting in a lasting alteration to my being. the seasons in our forest are ever-changing, but this winter inside will leave only frozen gates at my soul's entrance.

this winter world will pass, though it will not pass without leaving much dead in its path. now, i see the winter has gotten us both, like frost, spreading slowly and a great distance.

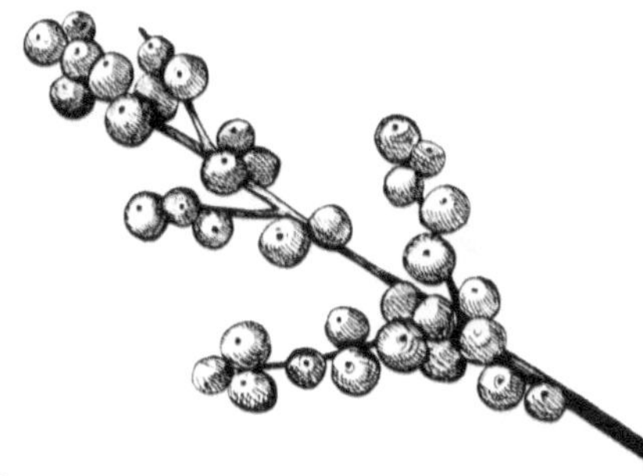

to heron

is there not a force
in your heart that demands
we continue, that demands
we don't let these naked trees
kill us? i hope it's there.

it has only been a month
of winter, but we are still.
i think the worst has passed;
i think we have endured
the strongest storms and
the whitest blizzards; i think
the heaviest weight of all
these winter-tears has
already bore down on us.

for even in the winter,
there are berries.

in time

we are no longer a team;
you do not provide for me
everlasting shelter
from winds of storms.
you do not give warmth
with your wings,
and you do not hold
the winter's tears
up from my spine.

no, instead, you lose
your feathers. instead,
you waste away. instead,
you let the wind take
from your beauty
and magnificence.
you give into the season's
bitterness; you are
not strong like me.

so i will go elsewhere
for my shelter and
elsewhere for my
warmth. i will find
in myself what
i always thought
i could find in you.

redbud

sweet heron,
it saddens me to see
us part, but i know
that our time together
was good and pure.
you cared for me,
and i cared for you;
i grew into a wonderful
creature underneath
the shade of your wings.
winter is ending,
and the new trees are
budding — i think
that spring is almost
here. i will never forget
about you and always
cherish everything
we had together,
but i see now something
new. it is time for
us both to live in
the spring instead
of this long winter.
i have discovered
we need different things
as life goes on,
and though my crown
drops in your absence,
and in the presence
of your memory,
i am ever grateful
for our many seasons
together.

at one time,
          the forest gave us
everything;
          but now it is spring.
                              i must come
                              out from the
          shade   of
                              your wings
                              and the shelter
of your greatness; i
must   drink   from
          the melted pond.
                              i must find the
          green grasses and the
                              places of the
          forest that   did not

          succumb
          to the long   winter
and   i must follow them
into the new   spring
season. this winter was
          lovely and
                    difficult and we
went through it
together but every
          winter
                    must

                              come
                              to an end.
          look, the redbuds are
                              already
                                        blooming.

to fawn

are you listening —
do your ears twitch
when i speak?
do the spots on your back
shift and roll?
strength from within
has been growing ever since
the winter starved us.
fawn, i am here.
it is me, from within.
listen to me:
i am growing stronger;
i am larger
than before.

spring

the spring is here
and for the first time
my bones have grown strong
enough to hold themselves up.
i do not need your warmth
or your shelter, but only myself
to survive. this winter
might have been long,
but my spots will still be
whiter than the winter
snow without you.

losing
me:

rape

I
about rape

let me tell you about rape
it is not like poison that eats the edges of something
and it is not like water that soaks the entirety
rape kills you from the inside out

rape is magma
it burns up what loves in your soul and leaves nothing behind
when it triggers
it is not like a rush of emotion that overwhelms and brings tears
it is the opposite

it is a quieting of emotions
a numbing
like ice
like grief
the same thing
if you think about it

rape punishes everything that thrives inside of you just for thriving
it steals compassion from its home
it extracts grace and ambition into the air
into another dimension
where they cannot peek through the cracks
or cry out

rape is like watching flowers grow in reverse
or seeing the way they flatten after a wild gust

rape is a great wind
it quiets a person the way silence falls over a town
and the people are left with sorting through what's been taken
and what's been destroyed

II
i only see absence

something is gone,
and my soul, in a great mess,
is so busy sorting through every item that has been scattered
that i don't even know what has been taken from me.
i can't even identify which items have been raptured.
for, like a small child, all i know is that there has been
a great destruction, and much has been lost.

III
rape is not

i cannot tell you what rape is
i can only tell you what rape is not
rape is not
an issue of forgiving
an issue of misunderstanding
an issue of wisdom
an issue of self-protection
an issue of self-esteem
an issue of broken religion
an issue of making the right choices
an issue of trust
an issue of mistakes
an issue of consent
an issue of intoxication
an issue of true love
an issue of priorities
an issue of self-care
an issue of self-control
an issue of patience
an issue of boundaries
an issue of letting him win
an issue of me

IV
rape is grief

on top of a candle, a wick stands tall.
each time this wick burns, a different flame crowns its head.
once thwarted, the same flame can't resurrect.
nothing can resurrect the feelings i have lost;
there is not giving, only saving for self.
the infinite fields of expansive trust are gone,
for, like a flame, they've been extinguished.
only a thin line of smoke rises in their place —
a fleeting shadow of what once was.

V

rape is like breaking up with yourself

heartbreak is leaving a person, and you end up taking a
piece of their soul with you.
rape is the opposite.
rape is like they took a piece of your soul with them —
they grabbed it from you.
you did not give it to them the way you would give
someone your soul when you're in love.
so instead, rape is like breaking up with yourself.
you can't get it back;
there is no closure,
and you take out the argument you might have had
on yourself instead.
everything feels like your fault,
but it hurts so much,
and you can't help but feel your body split in two.
you then have yourself and yourself.
both hate each other,
both love each other,
and these things cannot coexist,
which is why when rape happens to you,
your body can no longer feel like your own,
your soul can no longer feel like your own,
because if you were to force this coexistence,
you might collapse upon yourself and cease to be.

VI
my body is not mine

my body is not mine
maybe it used to be
maybe i once had possession of this hollow thing
not anymore
it is not mine the way that your arm is not yours after it has fallen
asleep in the nighttime
    my soul has fallen asleep in the nighttime
    this nighttime is not a hallucination i will never wake from
    but instead
    it is just a blistered reality
my body is not mine
but i am not afraid of it
although it needs to be returned to its rightful owner
    who
    do you think
    that is?

VII

my thief

there's a person in this world
that has something of mine.
this person decided in a moment
that they deserved me,
that they had rights to my emotional capacity.
not out of jealousy,
not out of practicality,
not even out of fear —
and here's where i get confused,
because i can't figure out why anyone would think
that they had a right to my soul.
for a long time, i didn't think anyone
could take my soul
without asking first;
rape changed my mind.

me, after

a corn stalk after a dust storm
a hollowed-out pumpkin
in mid-november
parts sunken in
wrinkles have found their way
into the skin
the edges have never been sharper
and neither have my cheekbones
but all you see is
i've lost twenty pounds
you're jealous
of my green figure
but you can't see
the reason

rape ate my insides
like maggots eat away
the insides of a vegetable
rape filled me
with a hollowness
it made me empty
and at the same time
too full
to even eat

intentionally blank

no music today
the rape is already too loud

an unsettling phrase that he said to me
after it happened

"it was nothing."

stitches

in my head,
they are red,
the stitches,
with black writing,
and i am plastered against the wall,
your hands pushing me
to its white, textured grains.
my eyes aren't blinking,
but you are taking,
taking,
taking.
each stitch has a title:
your name
your name
your name
your name
your name
your name
your name
seven in all
that sew my mouth shut.

blushing

i can feel it in my cheeks
the way i didn't used to —
now i know what it means
to blush.
i thought when you blushed
it was supposed to be
a happy feeling,
but for me,
blushing just means
all the bad memories have
travelled to my cheeks.

when we had no voice

thank you on behalf of us all —
every one of us
who has been taken
from the inside out —
when they were making casual
our darkest moments,
for saying something,
for standing up,
for making our pains your priorities.

what breaks

in particular order:
dawn
every bone
my ten-minute
a holiday
awkward silence
promises
the flower vase
me after you

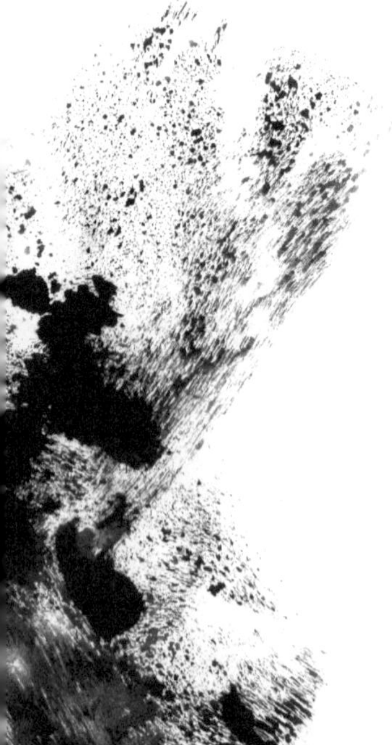

black and white

the color drains from my face,
from my whole body.
i am black and white.
not even the blushes
show pink,
not the eyes show brown.
when you took my soul
with this rape,
you took all my colors too.

vibrance

i hear that you are still breathing,
and over the course of three minutes,
three things leave me:
my soul,
my voice,
and all my colors.

intentionally blank ii

staring straight ahead
my soul is absent
as soon as i hear your name
i crumble
from the top down
i remember the feeling
of you taking it from me
and that violation
overtakes me
again
i cannot speak
there is nothing inside
just empty
cold
blank space

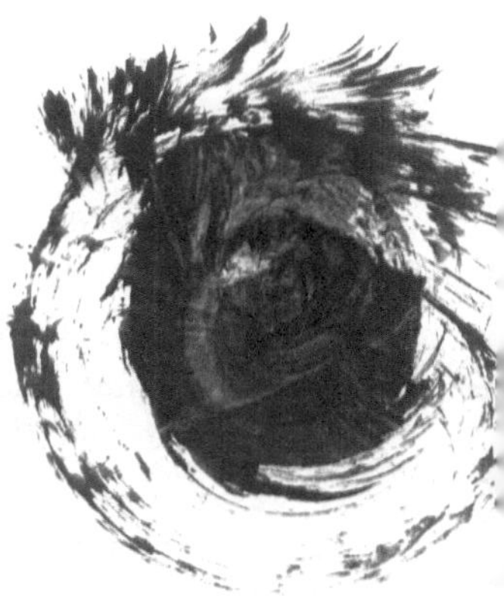

even when

you stayed ten steps ahead of me
as i walked to my car in "just a swimsuit" —
you thought it was unbecoming,
but we were leaving the pool

you didn't talk to me for one whole day
while you slept in my bed
and ate from my pantry,
after i said i'd leave you
if you slapped my ass again

you said no to my face
when i asked you to stop —
i did my best not to cry
as you took, took, took,
so as not to disgrace
your vast existence

and even then,
i thought i was falling for you.

but now

i was recently informed
that i have a right
to disagree
with your "preferences."
i want to yell,
scream, grab you
by whatever shred of dignity
you even have,
to look into your vacant eyes
and use every capital letter
to burn this message onto you:
You Do Not Treat Me This Way,
You Do Not Talk To Me This Way,
You Do Not Touch Me This Way,
and I Am Never Lifting A Finger
For You Again Because I Am
A White Rose, and You Are
Every Pelting Rain.

anna frazier

justice

to him:
the detective told me to stop talking
if i ever got uncomfortable.
but talking
is not what makes me uncomfortable;
not talking
is what makes me uncomfortable.
i tell you this:
there is not a stronger force
in my bones
than to talk
until every detail is written
every moment is spoken
every piece of my soul is bared,
for there is no greater power
that i can gain
than revealing your vast inconsideration.

rape is not a secret

i picture a darkness,
and then one candle lights.
i can see my own face in its dim glow.
i hold my candle up high,
not knowing who surrounds me.
i walk to the right a few steps,
exploring the environment.

out of this darkness,
my little sister runs to me.
she raises her candle to mine;
we hold them up for everyone to see.

continuing to walk, we pick up our pace,
and out of the darkness,
my childhood companion shows a candle's flame.
hers meets ours to make them brighter,
and we hold up our candles for everyone to see.

with haste,
we scavenge the atmosphere of hidden secrets,
and out of the darkness,
my dearest friend uncovers a light.
hers meets ours, now a torch,
and we hold them up for everyone to see.

our feet take us running throughout this barren place.
together we discover yet another.
out of the darkness,
a new friend shows her candle,
and we hold them up for everyone to see.

this is how i picture all of our secrets,
and the once small flame
that burnt within me,
that felt violated and betrayed,
that sought justice for myself,
transforms
into an unstoppable blaze
that engulfs my spirit,
that feels empowered and capable,
that seeks justice for all of us.

i run out of this picture
and into the police station,
and i tell
every detail,
every moment,
every broken piece of me
to someone with power
to act.

so,
rape is no longer my secret.
if it is yours,
then let it be yours
and no one else's.
but it couldn't be mine.

if it is your secret

i hope that my story
will illuminate yours
i hope that my mouth
will open yours
i hope that my courage
will spark yours
i hope that my chains
will unlock yours

anna frazier

the price of me

it was not easy
to run into the station,
to write four pages
of dripping betrayal.
it was not quick either,
nothing about it
was simple
but the price of me
is much more infinite
than the price i
pay to defend it.

processing the report: a series

november 8, 2:14pm

i am sitting here
in an elevated chair:
a shattered vase,
taped,
glued,
pieced back together —
but for some twisted reason,
i am wondering if you are okay.

what is that in me
that wants to make sense of you
before myself?

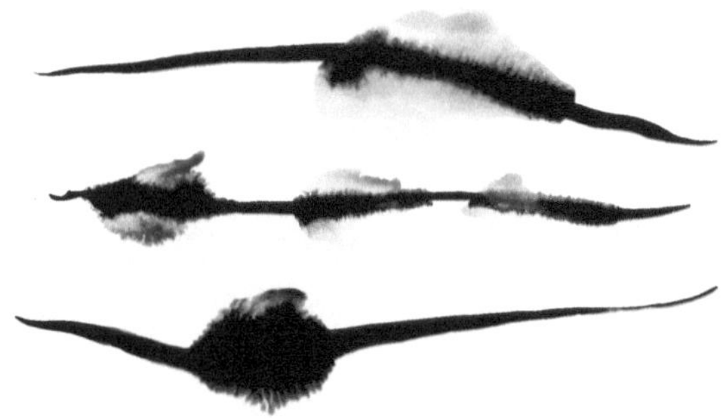

november 8, 2:24pm

i don't remember
whether you were
good or bad
to me.
i only remember
the falling in love,
the rape,
the disease,
and your absence.

november 8, 2:29pm

my soul is sick;
when i think
of you
i think disaster.

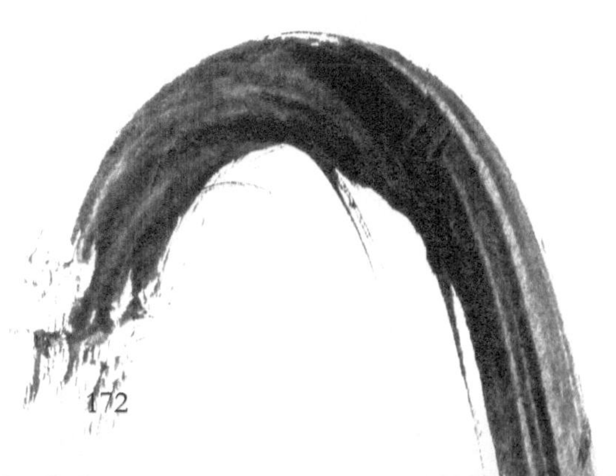

november 8, 2:41pm

i will see you soon.
the moths are turning;
they are unsettled by your name.
i try to soothe them, to tell them
you are safe, but still
their wings flap,
their darkness awakened
by the thought of an encounter with you.
i am certain they seek to
weigh me down,
so that i am unable to take
even one step closer.

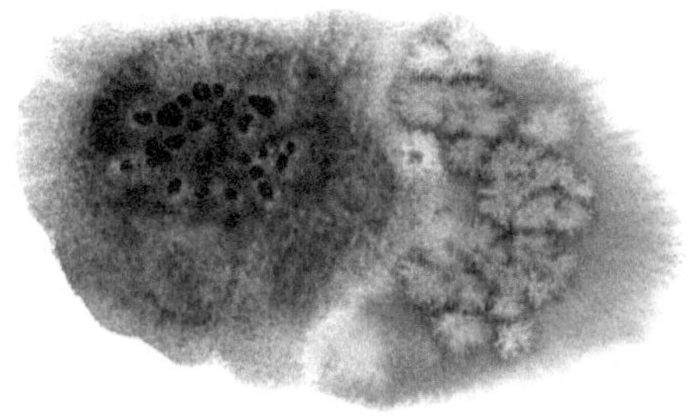

november 8, 2:42pm

dear you,

i am becoming
physically ill
and wondering
if this is
your effect
on my body.

sincerely,
my inevitable migraine

november 8, 2:46pm

when you ask me
why i went to the police
before i went to you,
all i will say is
"i had to hate you
before i could love myself."

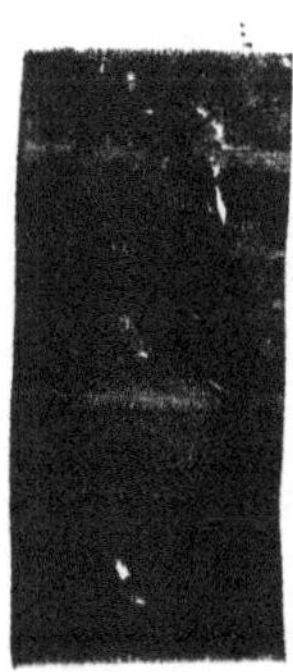

november 8, 3:02pm

i think i was simply terrified
of knowing
this great and horrible enemy
out there somewhere.
but now that you stand in front of me,
i see that you are human too,
and, like me, can also be defeated.

interface

all anyone can ever ask for
is the strength to do
what must be done
and the courage
to act on it.

reconciliation

i never wanted it to end.
for only two hours i felt okay —
not before and not after —
and i knew as soon as you left,
as soon as your green eyes turned away,
that the magic would fade,
and then,
it would just be me
and the rape.

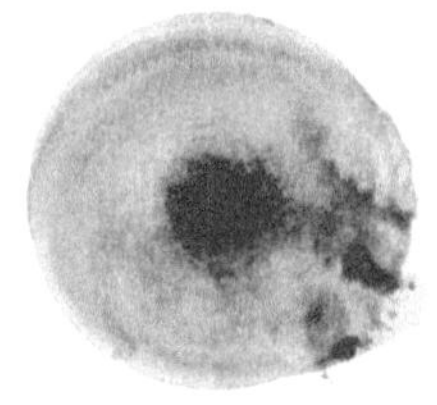

apology

i looked into your
green eyes, and i saw
everything:
i saw your heart,
i saw your sadness,
i saw your apology,
i saw the way you care for me,
and i saw the way that
you wished things weren't this way.

why I did what I did

in death,
there is freedom,
but also
a great sadness.

you see,
the end goal was not revenge,
but understanding.

wake

saying no

no.

undoing

anybody who tells me
i laugh too much
is ridiculous
there is no such thing as
laughing too much
so then
it is not me
that is too much
it is you
that is not enough

sometimes i fall apart again

not entirely like i used to,
but i get confused
by everyone's voices
all smashing against each other…
"time heals;" "let go;" "this is now;"
like it's something obvious and tangible, but
how do you let go when you didn't even know
you were holding onto something?
i don't know which way is up or down —
everyone has words but no one makes sense —
maybe i'll follow my intuition;
maybe i don't need permission
to listen to myself.

cycle of abuse: after anger

this rage is a burning fire,
but it comes out of me
a rushing river.

river of sorrows

sometimes i hear how angry you are
about the way he abandoned you,
and i remember how angry i am
about the way he abandoned me,
and i want to cry endlessly for us both,
which bleeds into
all the damage of the universe,
and then i want to cry
for that too,
and here i am
in a river of sorrows.

healing

i heard by God
that you can get
your soul healed.
i think i'd give
anything for that.

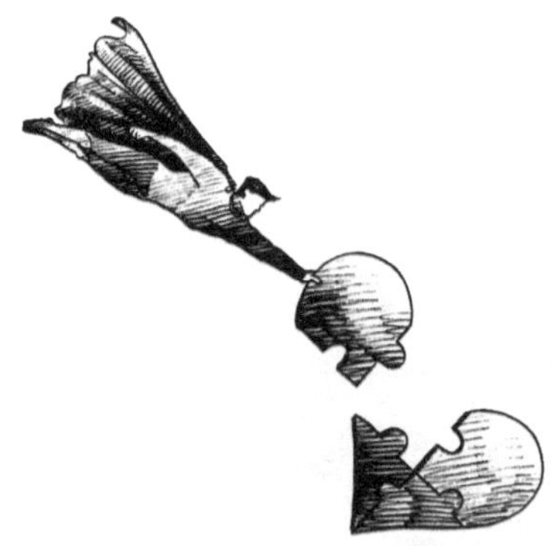

i lack nothing

He told me
i lack nothing
just because i exist,
so i continued
to repeat this to myself,
and eventually,
i believed
that i lack nothing
all by myself.

the human spirit

i have found that
the human spirit is
more resilient than an
ocean wave; fear
does not stop it
from standing
up to a storm.

resurrection

something grew back in me,
some small part that he
took away, some piece of my
dignity, some shred of my
self worth resurrected
when you
cared for me,
made me dinner,
asked for my opinion,
cried in my arms,
asked me to come closer,
looked back at me.

trust issues look different
on everybody

i am there
in your arms.
we are so close,
and yet,
my arms still fold
between my chest and yours.
i am not ready
to trust again,
even my arms know that.
i want to be close to you,
but for some reason
i won't let myself.
this is the same way
that when i am hungry
i can't seem to eat,
in fear that it might
alter the
almost-comfortable
feeling in my body.

ROAD
CLOSED

what helped

instead of hugs,
or tears,
or telling you everything,
i ate the pretzels you offered,
and for some reason,
that dissolved my worries.
i never knew
a childhood snack
could have so much power.

yes and no

yes to feelings
no to impulsive decisions
yes to being there when we need each other
no to using each other for selfish reasons
yes to taking things slow
no to jumping and blindness

the space between falling

i am in the space between falling:
a place filled with
the sound of Keeping My Distance
and the smell of two perfumes.
i see two spirits in this space:
the first, Possibility,
the second, Damage.
i gently acknowledge both
and turn to this feeling:
a gentle air that settles on my skin —
an air without pressure,
or obligation,
for neither has given,
but each has gotten.
in this place,
i have freedom
to stay or leave,
lay near or sit far.
the space between falling feels
protected from danger or risk,
like watching ducks on a pond,
so removed from all that pollutes this world.

i notice

i notice
when you
make sure i am warm,
tell me i don't have to finish that drink,
ask if i want the lights on,
leave the door open,
walk me home at three am,
call me darling,
take special care to put just the right amount
of sugar
and
cream
in my coffee;
i notice.

small moments

even just to look at you
has been difficult, because
your eyes are my very favorite color.
but now,
what a pleasure it is
to trust someone
enough to hold their gaze.

raspberry kisses;
i finally can look at you
without forgetting
everything.

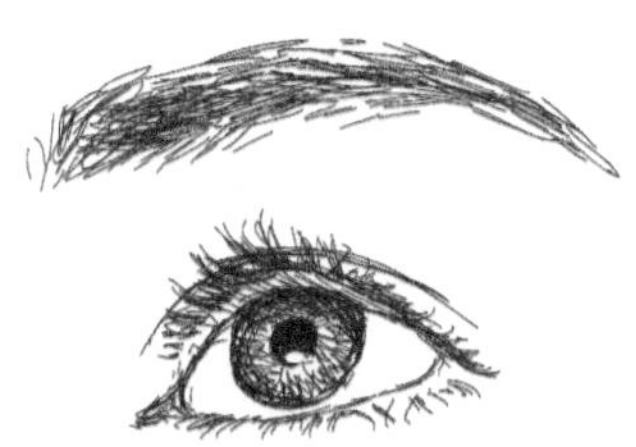

butterflies

i know this feeling
is unstable,
but please,
can i just rest here
in its presence
for as long as it will last —
it's such a relief
from every painful memory.

sunday

i'd never liked coffee so much
as the coffee i tasted while
we danced around the kitchen.
we switched cups
and thoughts,
and laughed about it all;
how silly the world is when i'm with you.

fine china

i tried to write
a poem about this moment
in all these varying
metaphors;
i couldn't do it.
so, i decided to write it
in english instead of
in poetry,
and so,
in english,
it is like
i am sitting,
and you are sitting,
and the screen is flashing,
and the dog is blinking.
you look at me,
you look at the dog,
you kiss the dog,
and before i can think,
your jade eyes
land on me;
your careful fingertips
hold my face
like fine china.
you take one sip,
not more,
and return me to
my saucer.

okay

i can't describe what it is
to be okay
in the arms of another person,
except to say that
it is a nice feeling
in the positive direction.

unneatness

i'm beginning to be okay with
the unneatness
of things,
the way that my head does not
fit exactly into the crevice
of your chest,
and the way that our lips,
when they do touch,
do not have a consistent rhythm.
after some time,
my perfectionism rests,
and
the parts of us that
do not always make sense
are the ones
i learn to enjoy.

just for me

this poem is just for
me;
not any one else
will see.
for me,
he has to have
pink lips,
rosy cheeks,
and
pretty eyes,
pretty eyes,
pretty eyes…
and he does.

the

constant

undoing:

putting

    me

  together

again

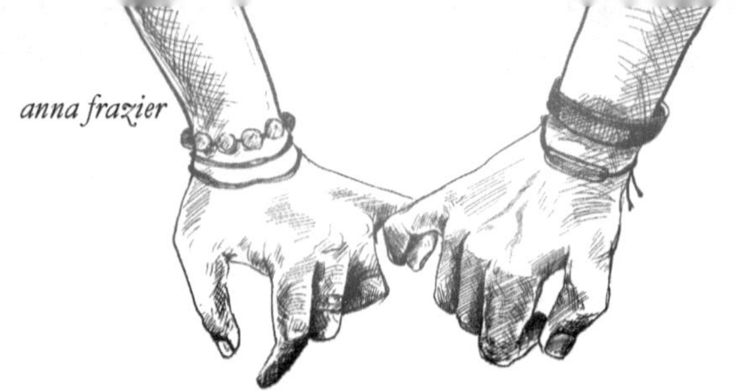

anna frazier

unity

why is it that things
don't become important to us
until we are a part of them?

expectations

why is there an expectation
that life will at some time
be less tiring,
more happy,
less tragic
and more magic?
where do these lies come up from?
maybe it is just our desire
to escape this terrible place.

i wonder

sometimes i want to ask questions,
but the way i was raised,
every question has an answer.
i'm not allowed to wonder,
because every answer is connected
by God,
every question
can be explained
by God,
every thought
is in the book
by God,
but,
by God,
can i just have
a moment where
i don't have the answer
and neither does He?

a story:
chapter one

i was standing behind them;
i could hear a man at the front.
he was large and well-spoken,
intelligent and commanding of the room.
everyone listened intently.
they leaned forward,
interested in what he had to say,
but i could not see the man,
and not seeing him made him harder to hear.

every year we returned,
and every year i grew a little taller,
but not tall enough.
i kept coming back, hoping to become tall enough,
but then i stopped growing.
i tried to see through the two
in front of me,
but they were so, so tall.
i thought they would notice
that i could not see
around them
but to my disappointment,
they did not move —
a shame
for such a tiny person to miss
such a big voice
because of two
people.

chapter two

away from them i stepped.
they asked, "where are you going?"
i told them, "away from you."
they appeared alarmed,
offended, even.
but i knew what the man was saying
was more important than
the two people.
i crawled between
the shadows
of many,
tall and short,
young and old,
withered
and not withered.
i crawled right up
to the man's heavy shoes.
i saw him,
i heard him,
and his wisdom
i swallowed.

chapter three

to them:
i'm sorry
i went from you.
i can't say
if i should be angry
that you stood
in my way,
but i can say
i'm not angry
that i found
my own.

tea

what is tea for
but to drain the feelings?
what is passion for
but to satisfy the soul?
what are words for
but to make connection
between what separates?
what, then,
are people for?

returning home

everyone says
they will go off
after college
to a new city or town,
to plant themselves,
to settle down.
but maybe i will stay here
for the rest of my life,
in a place where
all my pieces
came back together,
where i became
a whole person
when tragedy split me
into many.
even while it is not
a city with many lights
or tall towers,
it is the place where
i feel the most whole,
so maybe i will stay
for that reason
alone.

the feeling of my soul being pieced back together

words cannot express it —
her voice is like the ocean waves,
a mirror shattering
in reverse,
the sea's surface
showing the sunlight
where it came from.

for my best friend: the moment i unmissed you

my eyes looked for you
for minutes
and minutes.
they saw the people laughing
and drinking,
but they did not find you.
you came into view;
i looked at the floor.
before i knew anything,
my feet took me like wind to your embrace —
a fire, i consumed your body with mine;
like water you refreshed me
like the earth you grounded me
like the sun you made my face bright again
like the moon you calmed my spirit,
all in a single moment…
to you: thanks for everything.

magic soup

there's this magic
soup in my family
that fixes everything —
back aches,
heart breaks,
stomach pains,
broken brains,
existential sadness,
all the world's badness;
this soup fixes anything,
so i thought you might like
the recipe:

> *pastina*
> 2 c. chicken broth
> 1/4 c. celery
> 1/2 c. acini de pepe
> *boil dieci minuti
> per al dente pastina

reflection

i used to look at my life through
the bathroom window,
and see the stars, and the moon,
and think, *gosh,*
my future is out there somewhere…
and now i look out my bathroom window,
and i think, *wow.*
i remember the last time i looked
out this window.
things were so different…
i was young
and naïve
and had no idea about the world
outside of my nicely laid plans.
now everything is upsidedown,
and when i wake up tomorrow,
reality won't be better than my dreams,
but in time i think it could be.

what is forgiveness: a conversation

no way am i free.
freer, maybe,
than i was in the past,
but all that means
is time has passed,
and i've worked hard
to face my feelings.
it doesn't mean
i know how to let go.
      i don't think it's about
      "letting go" or "moving on"
      but more
      living in the present
      and
      being able to be
      the person you strive to be.
forgiveness is
forgiving yourself for having to go through shit.
maybe at least part of it…
      i agree completely.
not like, "let's move on,"
or "let's give this person another excuse,"
or "let's just be more loving to others."
it's more like,
"let's remember this happened,"
and
"let's remember our worth,"
and
"let's be more loving to ourselves."
      and again, i agree.

redemption

in the places i was empty, He filled me —
the ocean rose inside me once more.
He saw where i could not speak
and placed in me
a strong and beautiful voice;
now, rivers fall freely out of my mouth,
waves crash upon the cliffs of my eyes,
and, again, i can see every color.

november 8, 3:04pm

i have learned how to turn
coarse flour into bread
and
lingering thoughts into poetry.

why i write

to get through the day,
the hour,
to help people like you
get through the day,
the hour,
to show you how
i got through my darkest days,
my darkest hours,
to give you a reason to live
and tell you
that you have given me
a reason too.

epilogue

the aforementioned events live in the years they occurred. the depictions of people in this book are not full depictions of the people involved, but only moments and sides. the perspective given to you is one only of the writer and not of the others involved; therefore, it is a slanted perspective, nevertheless true to the writer at the time of its writing. since its writing in two-thousand eighteen, the writer's relationship with her father has been resolved. the other traumatic experiences detailed here have been worked through over years of therapy, and some are still being worked through, as they will continue to be. it is the writer's belief that trauma takes lifetimes to resolve and will never be forgotten but that it is possible to be healed and to eventually wake up and feel okay.

review

leave a review of this collection at annafrazierpoetry.com in the CONTACT section.

reviews help the author's collection to be viewable by a wider audience, so others can share the experience that you have just had reading the collection.

notes

Stuart Bache created the beautiful cover art.

Nicola Grigg created the drawing on 15.

Michael Thalman created the drawing on 57. visit
mthalmanart.com for more.

Sam Larson created the drawing on 108.

the words, "you are a rainbow: / enticing at first glance
/ but there's nothing to hold onto" are taken from
Lana Del Rey's song, "Get Free," referenced on 116.

other images are by various shutterstock artists.

acknowledgements

endless gratitude to my editors and mentors, Dr. Chloe Honum and Dr. Michael-John DePalma, for affirming my ideas and showing me the way, and to my closest friends and family for offering me support in my darkest hours. finally, thank you to my escape, the floor of the basketball court, for allowing me to come as i am, to compile my thoughts, to put this book, and myself, together.

maddie — you're the first person i showed my poems to. thank goodness for you and our meeting, as this book may have never come about. you gave me the courage to open my soul.

libby — lucky that i have you trudging through my mental health journey with me. you get me; i hope nothing about us ever changes.

frank — 221 is for you. day ones.

keum — thank you for supporting my passion for creating since the first day we met. your encouragement through my darkest hours has been extraordinary; you keep me going.

sarah — you complete me, and our mutual love for poetry brings so much joy into my life. you get me. i love you. check 224.

dad — thank goodness 78 came true.

nonna — grazie mille. ti amo. sinceramente, il tuo

biscotto duro. 222.

nikita gill — thank you for writing and being fearless in that task. reading *Your Soul Is A River* inspired me to write my own book of poetry, exposing issues that the world gives us no space to discuss.

index

www.ingramcontent.com/pod-product-compliance
Lightning Source LLC
Chambersburg PA
CBHW030903060726
47591CB00005B/1393